ENGLISH
Pupil Book 1

Tom Watt and Gillian Howell

RISING ★ STARS

Rising Stars UK Ltd, 22 Grafton Street, London W1S 4EX

www.risingstars-uk.com

Every effort has been made to trace copyright holders and obtain their permission for the use of copyright materials. The authors and publisher will gladly receive information enabling them to rectify any error or omission in subsequent editions.

All facts are correct at time of going to press.

Published 2008, Reprinted 2008
Text, design and layout © Rising Stars UK Ltd.

Story author: Tom Watt
Educational author: Gillian Howell
Publisher: Gill Budgell
Cover design: Burville-Riley Partnership
Design: Cambridge Publishing Management
Illustrations: Patrick Boyer, for Illustration, Ltd
Photographs: Getty Images

British Library Cataloguing in Publication Data.
A CIP record for this book is available from the British Library.

ISBN: 978-1-84680-298-0

Printed by: Craftprint International Ltd, Singapore

Rising Stars would like to thank Alan Sefton and Scott Cohen of Football in the Community for Arsenal Football Club for their help and support.

Contents

Unit

1. We are top of the league. 4
2. You helped get us there! 6
3. The best day of my life 8
4. Player report 10
5. Manager's plans – exclusive 12
6. Fran Watson's diary (1) 14
7. Dotun's letter home (1) 16
8. Come on lads. We can do it. 18
9. Shelby Town 1 Liverpool 1. 20
10. The Diamond vision (1) 22
11. Shelby Town 2 Manchester City 1 24
12. Town pass latest test. 26
13. Shelby Town FC 28
14. Shelby Town 1 Manchester United 6 30
15. Dotun's letter home (2) 32
16. The season starts now! 34
17. Fran Watson's diary (2) 36
18. Today's thread 38
19. Brave Shelby crash to Arsenal. 40
20. The Diamond vision (2) 42
21. A difficult situation 44
22. Dotun Odegbame out 46
23. Dotun's letter home (3) 48
24. Shelby Town's hero?. 50
25. Shelby Town 2 Spurs 1. 52
26. According to the skipper 54
27. Fran Watson's diary (3) 56
28. Newcastle United 1 Shelby Town 1. 58
29. Let's get out there and get stuck in!. 60
30. What a season!!! 62

SPORT

May 12th • Daily News

TOWN HIT THE BIG TIME ON PENALTIES

Skipper's spot kick takes Shelby to Premier League

Shelby Town will be playing in the Premier League next season. This amazing story had a fairy-tale ending at Wembley yesterday. Ten years ago, Town were playing non-league football. Now, they will be taking on the likes of Manchester United and Arsenal.

But it was close. Very close! A nail-biting Championship play-off final went to extra time and penalties. The hero was captain Dave Morgan, who kept his cool from 12 yards to see Shelby Town home.

'I knew I had to score,' the skipper said after the game. 'The lads have been great all season and I could not let them down. We did spot kicks in training on Friday, so we knew we were ready if it came to a shoot-out. This is the best moment ever for Shelby. It's the best moment ever for Dave Morgan as well!'

Manager Mick Diamond said his team had been nervous at first but got better as the game went on.

'After half-time, I felt only one team was going to win it. The lads gave me everything, like they have all season. Dave will get the headlines but they were all heroes today.'

Shelby Town chairman Ernie Carstairs ran on to the pitch at full time. Who can blame him? His dream has come true, ten years after he took over the club.

'We were playing against Moor Green and Worksop ten years ago. Now, it will be Shelby Town versus Chelsea and Liverpool. It proves that you can do anything if you try hard enough. Thanks to Mick and all the players. We will enjoy ourselves tonight. Tomorrow, we can start planning for the Premier League!'

Team Talk:
- Retell the story from the cartoon strip. Try to remember the detail.
- Does your team play in the Premier League? What was their most nail-biting moment?

Skills Practice 1

Find all the words in the first paragraph of the text ending in *-ing.*

Rewrite each sentence with a different word (it doesn't have to be an -ing word).

E.g. *This amazing (fantastic) story had a fairy-tale ending (finale) at Wembley yesterday.*

Skills Practice 2

Write out these sentences with correct capital letters and full stops.

a) shelby town will be playing in the premier league next season

b) the hero was captain dave morgan

c) the captain believes his team will have a great season

Find a sentence that ends in an exclamation mark.

Game On

Answer these questions with full sentences.

1. How long ago were Shelby Town playing non-league?
2. List the names of the chairman, the manager and the captain of Shelby Town.
3. What does the chairman mean when he says, '...you can do anything if you try hard enough'?
4. What does the manager mean when he says, 'Dave will get the headlines...'?
5. The team practised spot kicks on Friday at training. What other skills do you think they practised at training?

YOU HELPED GET US THERE!

Now Come and Watch Shelby Town Take On the Premier League!

Special Season Ticket Offers for the Best Fans in England!

The captain, Dave Morgan, the rest of the players and the boss, Mick Diamond, want you to get the message! Thanks to you all for the fantastic support you gave us on the way to Wembley.

Thanks for the fantastic support you gave us at the play-off final as well.

What a day! What a game! What a prize!

FACTS!

- Shelby Town's first-ever season in the Premier League.
- Just eight weeks away.
- We would never have got there without you.

Now we want to make sure our loyal fans don't miss a minute of the action as we take on the biggest clubs in the land.

SPECIAL OFFERS!

Between now and the end of the month, you can buy a Shelby Town season ticket at a special 'Loyal Town' price. And there are other special offers too, like great deals on family tickets. But remember, the sooner you book, the less you'll pay to follow Shelby's first-ever season in the best league in the world.

Season tickets start at just £299. *That's less than £16 a game.*
Junior season tickets start at just £149. *That's less than £8 a game.*

Buy before the end of June and make sure of your seat at Manor Park. Be part of Shelby Town history as Dave Morgan leads the boys out against Manchester United, Chelsea, Arsenal and the rest.

Kick-off is just two months away, so ring the Town ticket office today.

Team Talk:

🛡 Reread the 'Special offers!' paragraph.
Discuss words such as 'loyal', 'great' and 'best'.
How do these words make you feel?
What type of writing is this?
🛡 What are the fans like at your club?
Are they the best in England?

Skills Practice 1

a) Write out these words with the correct vowels.
- play _rs
- mess_ge
- min_te
- Pr_m__r Leag__
- s__s_n

b) Now write the correct versions of these words.
- tickt
- famly
- wrld
- munth
- soonr
- histry

Skills Practice 2

Write out the sentences and phrases below using correct punctuation.

a) Special Season Ticket Offers for the Best Fans in England

b) Be part of Shelby Town history as Dave Morgan leads the boys out against Manchester United Chelsea Arsenal and the rest

c) The manager says he is the special one

Write a sentence that includes a comma and an exclamation mark.

Game On

Answer these questions with full sentences.

1. What is the cheapest Shelby Town season ticket?
2. When does the new Shelby Town season start?
3. Why should Shelby Town fans buy a ticket before the end of June?
4. What does this phrase mean: 'We would never have got there without you'? What have the fans done?
5. Why does the leaflet say, 'Special Season Ticket Offers for the Best Fans in England!'?

Joe Watson   Summer Homework Topic
Year 8   July 5: The Best Day of My Life

I will remember the play-off final for ever. It was the best day of my life, from start to finish. It was the best day in the history of the team I support, Shelby Town.

We all went down in the car to Wembley together: me, my sister Fran, Dad and Dad's mate, Jim. It took us two hours to get there and two hours to find somewhere to park! It was worth it. Walking up Wembley Way and past the Bobby Moore statue gave me the shivers! Dad kept saying, 'I never thought I'd see the day.' There were more Town fans inside than I had ever seen before, all wearing their replica shirts, waving Shelby flags and singing. The noise didn't stop from the first minute to the last. The game just flew by and we should have won in normal time. The shoot-out was fantastic, though. What a way to win promotion! When Dave Morgan hit the winning penalty past their keeper, I thought the cheer was going to blow the roof off Wembley!

What a day! We sang all the way home in the car:

'And it's Shelby Town! Shelby Town FC! They're by far the greatest team the world has ever seen!'

We are in the Premier League at last. I have been counting the days until the new season starts. And yesterday the new fixtures came out. Our first game is against Liverpool at home. Who knows? Maybe that will turn out to be an even better day than the play-off final. That's if Dad or Jim can get hold of some tickets!

Come on the Town!

Team Talk:
- Think of five questions that you would like to ask Joe Watson about the best day of his life.
- What's your best ever day in football?

Skills Practice 1

Manager's Message
Suffixes go at the end of words to change their meaning.

Change the following words by adding suffixes (*-er*, *-est*).

- great
- small
- tall

Write a sentence for each using all three versions of the same word.

Skills Practice 2

Homophones are words that sound the same but have different meanings.

a) Write one sentence for each word.

- there/their/they're
- to/two/too
- by/buy
- knows/nose
- way/weigh

Find at least one word from each group above in Joe's essay.

b) Write out this paragraph and underline all the homophones.

The Shelby Town manager knows that there are two types of player. Some are too much trouble, but there are honest professionals. They're a joy to have in the team.

Game On

Answer these questions with full sentences.

1. Who went with Joe to Wembley for the play-off final?
2. What did they do on the way home?
3. Why does the writer say that 'Walking up Wembley Way and past the Bobby Moore statue' gave him the shivers?
4. Describe how the match ended.
5. Joe wants to get tickets for the first game of the new season. List the ways he could try to get tickets.

Player Report/Confidential

Player name:	**Dotun Odegbame (pron. Oh-Deg-Bah-Me)**
Date of birth:	**26 February, 1984**
Nationality:	**Nigerian**
Position:	**Striker**
Height:	**1.90m**

The player was seen playing for Benfica at home to Porto in Lisbon. Benfica played a 4-5-1 shape. D.O. was on his own up front. Benfica won 3-1. D.O. scored the first goal after 22 minutes. He came off 10 minutes from time with an ankle injury.

Analysis

Strengths: D.O. is a very tall striker. He has won fourteen caps for Nigeria. He has outstanding pace and good ability in the air. He is right-footed but scored his goal from 12 yards with his left foot. He has clever skill on the ball and a sure first touch. He passes the ball well. He looked willing to work hard for the team. He has been Benfica's top scorer this season.

Weaknesses: D.O. is a good athlete but not very strong. He may need help with his diet and must do more work in the gym. He was easily knocked off the ball twice early in the game. He sometimes tries long passes when a short pass would be better. Some of his runs made it hard for other players to find him. He did not seem used to playing alone up front. Benfica usually play two strikers. Nigeria always do.

Recommendation

D.O. is an exciting player and has an excellent goal-scoring record. His great strength is his pace, which we do not have up front at the moment. He looks as if he could score a lot of goals with his head. He would be a good target for our wingers, Smith and Dunne. He needs to be coached to time his runs better. He would need to be stronger in English football. If Benfica were willing to sell him for less than £1 million, I think D.O. is worth a gamble.

Brian Harris

Brian Harris (Chief Scout)

Team Talk:
- Discuss what 'confidential' means. What other documents are confidential?
- What are the strengths and weaknesses of your favourite player?

Skills Practice 1

Look at these root words from the player report. Make two more words using the root word.
Use different word endings.

E.g. *foot* —→ *football* —→ *footballer*

assist —→
pass —→
act —→

Game On

Answer these questions with full sentences.

1. How tall is Dotun Odegbame?
2. What is Dotun's great strength?
3. What was unusual about the goal he scored in Lisbon?
4. List at least three things that Dotun needs to improve.
5. Explain the words and phrases below and then think if they have a different meaning outside football.
   - knocked off the ball
   - up front
   - pass
   - coach
   - match
   - goal

Skills Practice 2

a) Reread the section of the report on Dotun's strengths. Rewrite it with different adjectives.

   E.g. *D.O. is a very impressive striker. He...*

b) Now write your own football sentence using powerful adjectives.

   E.g. *Manchester United's controversial new forward made a dynamic debut for the Reds with a delicate pass.*

Manager's Message
Use a thesaurus to help you find more adjectives.

(11)

◄ ► C + 🌐 http://www.shelby.premiumtv.co.uk/ Google

Logon   Contact A Creative   BBC NEWS | ... Front Page   Demon Inter...Mail: Login   eBay UK – T...Marketplace

Shelby Town FC

Home

News

Manager's page

Fixtures

Match reports

Online shop

Contact us

Manager's Plans – Exclusive

The new season is just a couple of weeks away. Shelby Town's stars have been back at work for three weeks now. Mick Diamond has had a busy summer organising training and looking for new players. In a web exclusive, Sandy Lane talked to the boss about getting ready for life in the Premier League.

Sandy Lane: Thanks for talking to us, Mick. How was training today?

Mick Diamond: No problem. The boys are doing really well. To be fair, they are excited about that first game against Liverpool. They all worked hard to stay fit over the holidays so they came back ready for the work we needed to do in pre-season.

Sandy: Is this pre-season very different from last year?

Mick: Not so different, really, because we have always been a fit team and we will be again. What will be new to most of the boys is how clever the top teams are. We have done a lot of work on keeping the ball. If you give it away in the Premier League, it can take a long time to get it back!

Sandy: Any news on new faces at the club?

Mick: Well, I want to say we think the boys who got us promoted can do a job in the Premier League. Look at Wigan and Reading a few years back. They did all right in the Premier League and without changing the team too much.

Sandy: But there have been rumours about transfers, like the Nigerian striker from Benfica?

Mick: We've got our eyes on one or two players including the boy Odegbame. But we won't pay over the odds for anybody. We aren't a club who can throw money away but we are looking to bring one or two in before the season starts. We aren't unhappy with what we've got but if we can find players to give us a bit extra, we will. As soon as we know for sure, we'll let the fans know. Trust me!

Sandy: Thanks Mick. We will!

Team Talk:
- 🛡 Look at the questions Sandy asks Mick. How are they different?
- 🛡 Does your team have a website? What would be on your club's website?

Skills Practice 1

Manager's Message
Pre- means 'before' so a prefix goes before the word to change its meaning.

In the interview Sandy asks Mick about the 'pre-season'.
Find the prefix *un-* in the text.
Add *in-*, *dis-* or *un-* to these words to change their meanings.

- happy
- allow
- attentive
- agree
- continue

Game On

Skills Practice 2

Connectives are words that join parts of sentences together.

Write out the sentences below and underline the connectives.

E.g. *It's not so different really <u>because</u> we have always been a fit team.*

a) We aren't a club to throw money away but we are looking to bring one or two players in before the season starts.

b) They did all right In the Premier League and without changing the team too much.

Now write your own four sentences using *because*, *and*, *so* or *but* once in each.

Answer these questions with full sentences.

1. How long have Shelby Town been back at work?
2. What are there rumours about?
3. When Mick says, 'I want to say we think the boys who got us promoted can do a job in the Premier League', why does he say, 'I want to say'?
4. What sort of things might the top teams do to be so 'clever'?
5. Who might be interviewed next on the website?

August 2007

3 Wednesday

Today, one of the best surprises I ever had. The start of the new season is only ten days away. Liverpool at home: Steven Gerrard, Pepe Reina, Fernando Torres! In the flesh! Playing Town at Manor Park! We've been following the news all summer. We signed a new striker, Dotun Odegbame, last week. I hope he's going to be worth all that money.

Anyway, me and Joe have been talking about going to the first game. Every time we asked Dad he said we'd talk about it later. Maybe he couldn't afford the tickets. Maybe they were already sold out. My brother and I were thinking we could put our savings together and see how much we had.

Then Jim came round after work today. After we'd had our sandwiches, we were talking about Town. Jim wanted to know if we thought Town could survive in the Premier League:

'Of course we can!' Joe said. I hope he's right. I'm not so sure.

Jim said, 'It will be good to see for ourselves, won't it?'

He was smiling when he said it. And then he took out two envelopes. One with 'Fran' on it and the other saying 'Joe'.

Inside each envelope was a ticket for Town versus Liverpool. We went mad. Joe ran round the kitchen like he'd just scored a goal. I did high fives with Jim and shouted out, 'Thank you!'

Dad was looking a little red in the face, like he didn't know what to say. Then Jim said to him,

'We've waited a long time to see Town in the Premier League, I wouldn't forget my best mate would I? You're coming too, Frank!'

He had got another ticket for Dad. The Bank Lane posse are all going together!

Team Talk:

- Talk about the informal and incomplete sentences in paragraph one and why these are used in a diary but not in other recounts.
- Text messages/postcards are often written as short sentences. Use complete sentences to recount a text/postcard you have received.

Skills Practice 1

Write out these sentences from the diary and add the correct speech punctuation, exclamation marks, question marks and full stops.

a) Of course we can Joe said
b) Jim said It will be good to see for ourselves won't it
c) I wouldn't forget my best mate would I You're coming too Frank

Skills Practice 2

Change the following two sentences into direct speech, using speech marks correctly as Fran did in her diary.

a) Blackburn's coach told me they are plagued with injuries.
b) He added they would still field a strong team.

Game On

Answer these questions with full sentences.

1. How long is it until the start of the new season?
2. What day was it when Jim came round?
3. Why do you think Jim smiled when he said, 'It will be good to see for ourselves'?
4. Find two ways in which Dad gives the impression he cannot afford the tickets.
5. Write a paragraph to describe Fran's family.

Dear Mum and Dad,

How are you? Well, I am here. The English club I told you about did a deal with Benfica and I am now a Shelby Town player. I had my first game yesterday. It was a friendly match against Lyn Oslo from Norway. Do you remember? Benfica played them in the UEFA Cup two years ago. I did not score yesterday but I got on well with my team-mates. We have a week now before the first big game — Liverpool in the Premier League.

I got to Shelby a week ago and the first days were hard. I must catch up on my fitness. There is a good spirit here. I enjoy speaking to the rest of the boys in English after three years in Portugal! This will be Shelby's first season in the Premier League but I think they have some good players at the club.

Dave Morgan is the captain and he has made me feel at home. The manager is good but he has a strange sense of humour. When things are good, he says they are bad. When things are bad, he says they are good. He keeps telling me I am useless but that means he is pleased with me. He makes us all laugh. He pretends he is still young enough to play and joins in with our five-a-side games. When he scores, he goes crazy. If someone tackles him, he always stops the game for a foul.

The club have paid for me to stay in a nice hotel. I am on my own here but I will find a house soon. Shelby is home for me now. I hope you will be able to come to England to watch me play. Miss you and everybody at home.

Your son,

Dotun

Team Talk:

🛡 Talk about the purpose of Dotun's letter. Is it to recount events? To reassure? To make a request? Does it have more than one purpose?
🛡 When would you write a letter home?

Skills Practice 1

> **Manager's Message**
> *And* and *but* can be used to join two clauses to make a compound sentence. Look for examples in Dotun's letter.

Use *and* or *but* to join these sentences and write out the new sentence. Explain your choice.

a) We are having a bad season. Gilberto is playing well.

b) I made a long pass. Matthews scored.

c) The light began to fade. We continued to play.

d) Dotun made lots of new friends. He missed his family.

Skills Practice 2

Use apostrophes to replace letters in these phrases: e.g. *I am here* becomes *I'm here.*

a) I had

b) I did not

c) We have

d) There is

e) This will be

f) He has made

Write this sentence using apostrophes to replace letters.

He is feeling confident there will not be a problem about his new contract with United.

Game On

Answer these questions with full sentences.

1. What sort of match was the first that Dotun played for Shelby Town?
2. How long has Dotun been at Shelby Town?
3. Why were Dotun's first days hard?
4. Had Dotun played against Lyn Oslo before? Explain your answer.
5. Write three things that Dotun may feel about staying in a hotel.

August 13
Come on lads. We can do it.

Shelby Town skipper Dave Morgan stood up. He looked slowly around the dressing room. It was five minutes before kick-off. This was the team's first-ever game in the Premier League. Dave could see worried looks on the faces of the other players. That was no surprise because their opponents were Liverpool. Dave looked calm even though he felt nervous. He took a deep breath. He'd been thinking about this all summer. Now he had something important to say to the boys.

'Well, lads, this is it. We battled all last season to be here. This is our chance in the biggest league in the world. I hope you're all looking forward to it. I am. The Liverpool team are next door, getting ready. They're a famous club with a team full of star players. I don't have to tell you about Steven Gerrard, Pepe Reina and Jamie Carragher, do I? Great players. But if we're scared of them, we'll lose today. I don't want that to happen. This is the moment we've been waiting for all our lives, isn't it?

'We might be worried about them, but they should be worried about us, too. Nobody thinks little Shelby Town can beat Liverpool, so the pressure is all on them. They don't know anything about us, do they? They don't know Dotun can score like Didier Drogba. They don't know Danny is even faster down the wing than Theo Walcott. They don't know that when I tackle somebody, he stays tackled! They don't know about our team spirit either.

'If we believe we can win, then we're halfway to winning. We're not in the Premier League to get autographs, are we? Come on lads. We can do it. Let's get stuck in!'

Dave clapped his hands loudly. His team-mates cheered. No one was feeling scared now!

Team Talk: 🛡 'Nobody thinks little Shelby Town ...'
How do you think this statement can motivate the team?
🛡 What does your coach say to motivate your team?

Skills Practice 1

Use *because* or *even though* to link these sentences. Write out the new sentence. Explain your choice.

a) We will win. We are better than them.

b) He enjoyed the game. It had a good atmosphere.

c) He got a red card. He kept arguing.

d) He kept playing. He was injured.

e) They couldn't go. They had no tickets.

Skills Practice 2

Write a short sentence to describe the main point of each paragraph in the text opposite.

E.g. *Paragraph 1 sets the scene.*

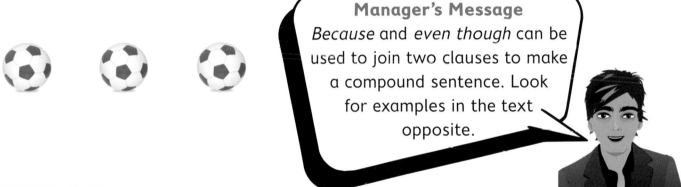

Manager's Message
Because and *even though* can be used to join two clauses to make a compound sentence. Look for examples in the text opposite.

Game On

Answer these questions with full sentences.

1. Who were Shelby Town's opponents?
2. How long was it until the start of the match?
3. Write two sentences to show the contrast between Liverpool and Shelby Town.
4. 'They don't know anything about us, do they?' What advantage does this give Shelby Town?
5. Describe how you would be feeling after the captain's talk if you were in the team.

Just a couple of minutes to go here at Manor Park and it looks like Liverpool will start the season with an away win, Chris.

Alan, I have to say that Shelby have given this quite a go. Since Alonso scored, they have kept Liverpool's attack very quiet. Mick Diamond can be proud of his players even though it may be too late to get anything out of the game. They're losing 1-0 but they haven't been outplayed.

Our first live game of the season on Five Live and it's been a good one. As you say, Shelby are still working hard to get back on terms. The ball's with the right back, Steven Jones. He plays it forward, looking for Smith, but it hits Riera. That's out for a Town throw, just short of the halfway line.

Ooh, I think Riera felt that. That hit him right where it hurts. I can see his eyes watering even though we're fifty yards away! Ouch!

Well, Shelby aren't in the mood to wait around. Throw-in quickly taken. Dave Morgan has got the ball on the edge of the centre circle. Now, here's Smith, taking on Finnan. I think we'll hear a lot more about young Danny Smith this season. Oh, and he's away from Finnan. Look at him go.

He needs to pick out the right pass now, Alan.

Smith looks up, swings the ball towards the Liverpool penalty spot. Odegbame's got in between Agger and Carragher, here. Onto his head. Yes! Down into the corner. Nothing Reina can do about that. It's the moment Manor Park's been waiting for. What a goal on his debut! What a moment for Shelby Town! Odegbame with the equaliser. Seconds to go and it's Shelby Town 1 Liverpool 1.

Fantastic goal, Alan. They bought the boy for less than a million and he's already brought the crowd to its feet here. Perfect cross, perfect header. Exactly what Shelby Town needed and exactly what they deserve!

Team Talk:
- Take turns to read the radio commentary using expressive voices.
- What is the difference between radio and TV commentaries?

Skills Practice 1

Choose the correct word for the spaces in the following sentences.

bought or *brought*
a) When the new striker was _____ it broke the record for transfer fees.
b) He _____ a new, competitive spirit to the team.

our or *are*
a) If we _____ to win, we must raise _____ game.
b) _____ fans _____ the best!

quite or *quiet*
a) Suddenly the crowd went _____.
b) Someone started whistling, then _____ a few others joined in.

Game On

Skills Practice 2

Imagine the game is to be shown again at a later date. Rewrite each phrase as a formal sentence for new commentators.

a) Throw-in quickly taken.
b) Onto his head.
c) Down into the corner.
d) Nothing Reina can do about that.
e) Perfect cross, perfect header.

Manager's Message
A live commentary is unscripted and therefore contains informal uses of language and incomplete sentences.

Answer these questions with full sentences.

1. Where is the match being played?
2. What position does Steven Jones play and for which team?
3. What does the commentator mean when he says, 'Look at him go'?
4. Who does the commentator mean, and what happens, when he says, 'It's the moment Manor Park's been waiting for'?
5. In your experience, what else might bring a crowd to its feet?

Match-day programme Shelby Town v Manchester City, August 28, Kick-off 4.00

August 28

The Diamond vision

Welcome to Manor Park for our second home game in the Premier League. Welcome to the players, officials and fans of Manchester City Football Club. And welcome to the Sky TV cameras. It's going to be another big day for Shelby Town. We're going to try to make sure it's one to remember!

I believe in looking forward but I have to look back to the Liverpool game. I was proud of the players, who refused to give in. Our fans were fantastic that afternoon as well. You kept urging the lads to get forward. Your support made all the difference. Hopefully it will this afternoon, too.

It has been a difficult start for us. We know it will take time to get used to playing at this level. I believe in the boys, though. They have to believe in themselves. We were beaten at Ewood Park by a very good Blackburn team. There won't be many sides who will be able to win there this season.

It also looked bad for us at Upton Park when we went a goal down just before half-time. But the fight-back against West Ham the other night proved we have nothing to fear in the Premier League. At 2-1 I thought we were about to win our first game, but Mark Noble had other ideas! He took his goal well and 2-2 was a fair result.

In all our games so far we have been able to compete. Now we have to prove we know how to win. Manchester City will try to stop us. So will Mark Hughes. For me personally it's an honour to pit my wits against a manager of his experience. But now it's up to our two teams to fight it out.

Thanks again for your support. It really does make the difference. I hope you'll have a win to cheer at the end of the game.

Up the Town!

Mick Diamond

Team Talk:
🛡 Look at paragraphs three and four. What does the manager tell you about the matches?
🛡 Think of a question you would like to ask him about each paragraph.

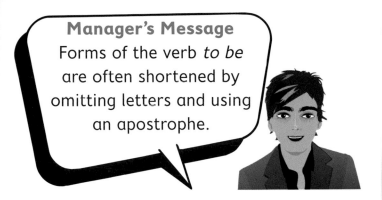

Manager's Message
Forms of the verb *to be* are often shortened by omitting letters and using an apostrophe.

Skills Practice 1

Rewrite these shortened verbs without using apostrophes.

E.g. *We're going to the big match.*
We are going to the big match.

a) He's a big fan.
b) You'll be lucky to score.
c) They're sitting on the bench.
d) I'm delighted to welcome you to our ground.

Skills Practice 2

If you can add 'by someone' or 'by something', it is a passive verb form.

Are these phrases *Active* or *Passive*?
a) We were beaten.
b) He was fouled.
c) I am going.
d) The fans are being thanked.
e) They were looking.
f) A penalty was taken.

Change these sentences from active to passive.
a) Spurs beat Wigan.
b) Injuries have dogged Owen for months.

Game On

Answer these questions with full sentences.

1. How many games have Shelby Town played at home in the Premier League?
2. Who beat Shelby Town at Ewood Park?
3. How many games have Shelby Town played since the Liverpool match?
4. What was Mark Noble's 'other idea'?
5. How can Shelby Town prove they can do more than just compete?

Richard Keys: Welcome back to Sky Super Sunday. Still to come this afternoon. On Sky Sports One and Sky Sports One HD, action from La Liga. It's Real Madrid versus Barcelona. Thierry Henry in great form for the leaders. Van Nistelrooy back for second-placed Real. Don't miss that. Kick-off at 8pm. And I know you won't want to miss next Sunday here on Sky: Manchester United versus Chelsea. Not a title decider but something close, even less than a month into the season.

Back to today and it's been a great afternoon for Shelby Town at Manor Park. They've beaten Manchester City 2-1. Geoff Shreeves is with the Barclays Man of the Match.

Geoff Shreeves: Thanks, Richard. I'm in the tunnel here with Town's French midfielder, Pierre Vert. Well done, Pierre. It doesn't come much better than that, eh?

Pierre Vert: Pardon me?

Geoff Shreeves: A win for your team and you score the goal that counts. Not a bad afternoon?

Pierre Vert: Ah, sorry. A very good afternoon. It is great to score but most important is what you call in England the three points!

Geoff Shreeves: It wasn't easy, was it?

Pierre Vert: The game wasn't easy. City are a good team, aren't they? Mr Hughes has them well organised. But my goal? That was easy! Dotun Odegbame did all the hard work. I just had to get into the box. He played a very good pass, didn't he?

Geoff Shreeves: He did indeed. But for all your hard work in midfield, as well as the goal, you are the Barclays Man of the Match. Well done. Back to you, Richard.

Richard Keys: Thanks, Geoff. And well played Pierre Vert. He earned that award this afternoon, didn't he? Non-stop running as well as the goal. We'll talk about the game in a moment with Jamie and Paul in the studio. And we'll hear from manager Mick Diamond as well. It's a first-ever win for Shelby Town in the Premier League. Don't go away!

Team Talk: 🛡 Summarise the text here in three sentences.
🛡 Use the cartoon strip to help you.

Skills Practice 1

Find and list all the words in Richard Keys' opening speech text that have a long *ee* sound.

Group them by their spelling patterns like this:

ee	ea	e-e
been	leaders	here

Game On

Skills Practice 2

Both Geoff Shreeves and Pierre Vert say that the game wasn't easy.
This is a negative statement.
A positive way to say it is '*... the game was hard.*'

Change these negative phrases into positives, e.g. *It wasn't easy* becomes *It was hard/difficult.*

a) It wasn't wet.
b) They weren't hot.
c) It isn't far.
d) It's not complicated.

Manager's Message
Use a dictionary to help you if you need to.

Answer these questions with full sentences.

1. Why was Pierre Vert being interviewed?
2. By how many goals did Shelby Town win the match?
3. Why do you think Pierre Vert said, 'Pardon me?' in the interview?
4. How did Dotun contribute to the win?
5. Who do you think will be interviewed next? Why?

SPORT

September 25th • Daily News

TOWN PASS LATEST TEST

Middlesbrough 0 Shelby Town 1 (Morgan 72)

Dave Morgan's smile was as wide as the River Tees last night. No wonder. The Shelby Town skipper has made a career out of stopping goals. Now he's scoring them too! The winner at the Riverside against an injury-hit Boro was his second in as many games. And was enough to earn Shelby their first away win of the season.

For most of the first half Morgan was busier in his own penalty area. Boro peppered the Shelby goal with shots, but the closest they came to scoring was when Stuart Downing's effort hit the heel of a Town defender. The ball spun up against the crossbar and bounced down. Morgan was happy to hack it off the line to safety.

'Sometimes you need a bit of luck in football,' said Morgan afterwards. 'We had to work very hard today. You know what they say: the harder you work, the luckier you become!'

There was nothing lucky about the winning goal. Odegbame won Town a corner on the left. Smith took it and Morgan found himself unmarked at the far post. The captain planted the simplest of headers into the corner. When Chris Riggott limped off soon after, the game was up for the home side.

'I told the lads before our first game we weren't in this league to collect autographs,' beamed a happy Dave Morgan. 'But I have to admit I didn't expect I'd be collecting goals for myself either!'

The experts who were writing Town off will have to think again. This was another test for Morgan's men, another test the Premier League new boys passed with flying colours.

We were lucky!

Odegbame won a corner

The simplest of headers!

Team Talk:
- How does this newspaper report and interview of the match differ from the television account and interview in Unit 11?
- Do you read football reports in a newspaper? Why/why not?

Skills Practice 1

Copy and complete these sentences using the underlined word with a suffix.

a) The first goal was simple but the second was _____.

b) All three players are fast but Jones is the _____ .

Add a suffix to these verbs to change them into nouns.

a) run

b) score

c) play

Skills Practice 2

Add a suffix to change the tense of these verbs.

a) *play*: Chelsea are _____ their last match today.

b) *watch*: We _____ the Manchester City match on TV.

Find all the words in paragraphs 2 and 3 of the text with the suffixes -*er* and -*est*.
Write their root words.

> **Manager's Message**
> Suffixes are very useful. They can change a verb to a noun (win/winner); change a verb tense (pass/passed/passing) and make comparisons (easy/easier/easiest).

Game On

Answer these questions with full sentences.

1. Where did Dave Morgan play for most of the first half?
2. Who took the corner for the winning goal?
3. Why was the game up when Chris Riggott limped off?
4. Why is it unusual for Dave Morgan to score a goal?
5. Write an explanation of the saying 'The harder you work, the luckier you get.'

Shelby Town FC

Matchday Schedule: Wednesday October 19

Luton Town versus Shelby Town, Carling Cup Round 4 Kenilworth Road KO 7.45pm

08.30: **Breakfast** available at training ground until 10.00.

09.30: All coaching and match staff to meet at training ground. **Planning meeting** in manager's office.

10.30: **On time, please!** Players assemble at training ground.

11.00: **Light training**. To include 15 minutes Youths versus First XI (Youths to line up as Luton Town). Confirm starting XI and substitutes. **Injured players to remain at training ground for treatment.**

12.00: Lunch at training ground.

13.00: **Coach departs** from training ground for Luton. **No mobile phones on coach, please!**

15.30: Via M6/M1. Arrive at hotel (Holiday Inn Luton South)

16.00: **Players rest**. Use of leisure club has been arranged. Ten twin rooms booked. Kit, etc. to be taken to ground. Report back to manager on condition of pitch.

17.30: Meet in Borders café for **pre-match meal**. Menu as per booking.

18.00: **Team meeting** in Bagley Suite. Whiteboard and DVD player booked.

18.30: All players and staff to depart hotel. **On time, please!**

18.45: Arrive Kenilworth Road

19.45: **Kick off Luton Town v Shelby Town. WIN!!!**

Shelby Town FC

Team Talk:
- Talk about the purpose of the schedule.
- Why do they need a schedule?
- What might happen if there were no schedule?

Skills Practice 1

Manager's Message
Recounts use past tense verbs.

Rewrite these sections of the schedule in complete sentences as a recount of what happened.

a) Planning meeting in manager's office

b) Lunch at training ground

c) Coach departs from training ground for Luton

d) Meet in Borders café for pre-match meal

e) All players and staff to depart hotel

Skills Practice 2

Write a synonym for each of the following words in the text:

a) staff   **d)** rest

b) assemble   **e)** condition

c) versus   **f)** depart

Rewrite and then underline the connectives that are to do with time in this paragraph, and the verbs that use the past tense.

Before moving to their new stadium, Bolton Wanderers were based at Burnden Park. They won the FA Cup four times, first in 1923 and finally in 1958 when they beat Manchester United 2-0.

Game On

Answer these questions with full sentences.

1. Who is meeting at the training ground at 9.30?
2. How much time has been allocated for light training?
3. Which of the scheduled activities can players choose to do?
4. Why might mobile phones not be allowed on the coach?
5. Is it important that all players and staff depart the hotel on time? Write a sentence to explain why.

November 13
Shelby Town 1 Manchester United 6

Mick Diamond came into the dressing room and shut the door. The players looked up at him. They sat on benches around the room. Boots and tie-ups were scattered on the floor. There was absolute silence. Nobody said a word. Everyone was waiting for the manager's reaction to what had just happened. Finally, Mick took a deep breath and began,

'6-1 at home. I've never taken a beating like that. Not as a player. Not as a manager. It hurts, doesn't it?'

One or two players bit their lips. The boss had asked a question but he didn't want an answer. Instead, he carried on,

'Maybe you think I'm going to go mad at you. But think about it. If you were bad players, I'd be shouting at you. If you'd played badly, I'd be shouting at you. If you hadn't worked hard enough, I'd be shouting at you. Our fans would have been, too. But what happened at the end of the game? They didn't boo you, did they? They clapped Manchester United off the pitch.

'Our supporters know football. They saw us get beaten by a team that would have beaten anybody. United looked like the best team in the world today. What can you do when Rooney and Ronaldo are in the mood like that? It's the first time all season we haven't given the other lot a game. I'm just glad we don't have to play United at Manor Park again this season!'

The players laughed with relief. They knew he was right. Mick put his hand up for quiet.

'I'm proud of you. We're halfway up the table and we're two games away from Wembley in the Carling Cup. I'm giving you two days off. Go home. Spend time with your families. I'll see you on Wednesday and we'll start getting ready for Villa next weekend. And then the semi-final the week after. We got taught a lesson today. Let's just make sure we learn from it, eh?'

Team Talk:

🛡 What is the effect of the short, simple sentences in the opening paragraph? How does the atmosphere change by the end?

🛡 What is the purpose of the manager's speech?

Skills Practice 1

Find and list all the words in the text opposite that have different long vowel sounds.

Group them by their long vowel sound like this:

/ay/	came, players, they
/ee/	deep
/ie/	Diamond
/ow/	nobody
/oo/	room

Skills Practice 2

Find and copy all the words in the text with the *ou* vowel spelling pattern.

Find three different 'ou' sounds in the text opposite that use the letters *ou* like this:

E.g. *City's new **ground** is easier to get to, so we **thought** the crowd **would** be bigger.*

Game On

Answer these questions with full sentences.

1. What had just happened before Mick Diamond's team talk?
2. Where were the players while Mick was speaking to them?
3. Why were Manchester United clapped off the pitch?
4. Who does Mick mean by 'the other lot'?
5. How do you think the players feel at the end of the manager's speech? Why?

Dear Mum and Dad,

How are you? I know we talk on the phone but I like to write as well.

It is great news that you can come to England at Christmas. It seems like a long time since we saw each other. I'm having a good time here. I want you to see for yourselves!

It's only a few months since I signed for Shelby Town but I am already feeling at home. The club is very friendly and so are the supporters. People are always stopping me in the street to say 'Well done!' or 'Good luck!' I don't know them but they treat me as if I was a friend.

The big news is that we are into the semi-final of the Carling Cup. We had a great game on Tuesday against Leeds United. They are a big club but not doing so well now. Even so, it was a close game. I scored in the first half and then we defended more and more. When the game finished it felt like we had already won the Cup! All the boys came and jumped on me because I had got the winner!

Coming home on the coach was such a good feeling. Our fans were tooting their horns when they came past us on the motorway. The manager, Mick, was very happy and said he was proud to be our manager. He always says that. I think he was a little bit drunk but that's OK. It was an important win for the club. They are glad I'm here. I'm glad I'm here too.

In the semi-final we play Everton a very strong team. Nobody thinks we will win but why not? It's two games and we play them at our ground first. That's not until New Year, though. It's crazy here. We have four games in eight days to play at Christmas time. You can come to watch, of course, but I hope we will have some time together as well!

Let me know when you will arrive.

Your son,

Dotun

Team Talk: ● Think of three different words or phrases to describe how Dotun feels.
● Have you scored a winning goal? How did you feel?

Skills Practice 1

Find and write down three nouns in Dotun's letter with the *-er* ending.

Write as many nouns as you can for what someone is or does ending in *-er*.

E.g. *plumber*

Skills Practice 2

Add the suffixes *-ed* and *-ing* to these verbs:

a) play

b) stop

c) watch

d) travel

e) score

Write all the words ending with *-er*, *-ed*, *-est* and *-ing* in the following sentence.

Blackburn's manager played his strongest team, but the visitors attacked from the start and ended as the winning side.

Manager's Message
Check if you need to add a consonant or lose a vowel at the end of the word.

Game On

Answer these questions with full sentences.

1. When are Dotun's parents coming to see him?

2. What was the last match that Shelby Town played?

3. Give two examples of why Dotun has 'such a good feeling'.

4. Why does Dotun say, 'We play them at our ground first'?

5. Does Dotun think he will see a lot of his parents when they visit? Give a reason for your answer.

http://www.shelby.premiumtv.co.uk/

Shelby Town FC

STFC

- Home
- **News**
- Manager's page
- Fixtures
- Match reports
- Online shop
- Contact us

THE SEASON STARTS NOW!

It's been a roller coaster ride for Shelby Town. We have held our own in the club's first season in the Premier League. We've reached the semi-finals of the Carling Cup, another first for Town. The FA Cup, though, wasn't so happy. All the build-up and a packed Manor Park but Spurs were too good for us. Good luck to them in Round Four at Anfield.

The season's been as exciting for the players as it's been for the fans. In a web exclusive, Sandy Lane talks to Town left back Peter Ball about the story so far.

Sandy Lane: Are you still down about last Sunday, Peter?

Peter Ball: We never got started. The early goal and then the injury to Mickel. Spurs had an easy time, really. We're sorry for the fans that came and were disappointed.

Sandy: Mickel must be very low.

Peter: He's doing OK. He's a brave keeper and you always run that risk. He's just thinking about getting back before the end of the season. The boss did well to get Jim MacDonald in on loan from Scotland so quickly. We don't know how long he'll be here but we know he can do a job for us while Mickel is out.

Sandy: How do you think things are going, the FA Cup aside?

Peter: Well, I can only speak for myself. But I'm enjoying every minute. It's been a dream to play in the Premier League and we're proving we deserve to be here. Apart from Man United, nobody's really outclassed us. We have to keep working now. All that matters is staying up.

Sandy: And the Carling Cup? Town's first-ever semi-final?

Peter: I don't even want to think about it! Shelby Town at Wembley again? Let's just say we're looking forward to Everton coming here next week for the first leg!

Sandy: So are thirty thousand Shelby fans, Peter. Good luck!

Team Talk:
- What does the phrase 'roller coaster ride' mean in this context?
- Can you think of other football-related phrases that are not really true?

34

Skills Practice 1

Rewrite these phrases without using apostrophes and then finish each sentence.

a) It's been
b) We've reached
c) wasn't so happy
d) The season's been
e) We don't know
f) Let's just say

Skills Practice 2

Copy out these phrases. Underline the ones that contain an apostrophe showing possession.

E.g. *Shelby Town's goal*

a) This season's games
b) The season's ended
c) The team's achieved a lot
d) The team's achievements
e) The manager's speaking
f) The manager's speech

Put the apostrophes into this sentence.

Derbys midfielders werent playing upfront enough.

Game On

Answer these questions with full sentences.

1. Who beat Shelby Town in the FA Cup?
2. What position does Mickel play for Shelby Town?
3. What does Peter mean by 'It's been a dream ...'?
4. What will happen if Shelby Town beat Everton?
5. How is Peter feeling about the semi-final? Use powerful adjectives.

January 2008

26 Thursday

I can't believe it! We're going back to Wembley. Shelby Town in the Carling Cup Final. What a way to start the New Year!

Last night was amazing. We couldn't go to Goodison Park. But me, Joe, Dad and Jim went down to Manor Park to watch the game on a big screen. We were only 1-0 up from the first leg, so nobody thought we could go through. Not even Joe, who always thinks we'll win.

Everton bombed forward right from kick-off but we held out. Jim MacDonald made a couple of great saves. I didn't want to look! It stayed 0-0 in the second half and we even hit the post. But ten minutes from the end, Tim Cahill scored for them and it went into extra time. Dad said,

'They've got the crowd behind them now. I think we're in trouble.'

I didn't say anything but I thought he was right. Then, just a couple of minutes into extra time, Leon Osman fell over in the box. Joe and everybody else shouted out,

'Dive! It was a dive!'

But you could see on the replay that Dave Morgan had fouled him. Osman scored the penalty and we were just hanging on for a few minutes into injury time, and Jim said,

'Never mind. They played their best, didn't they?'

But just as he said it, Danny Smith shot from the edge of the area and the ball hit a defender. Tim Howard dived the wrong way and the ball bobbled in. 2-1 to Everton but we had an away goal and when the whistle blew we had done it! Everybody at Manor Park went mad, hugging each other and screaming. It was the best night ever!

WE'RE GOING TO WEMBLEY!

Team Talk: 🛡 Talk with a partner about what you would write in your diary about the match.
🛡 How would it be the same or different?

Skills Practice 1

Rewrite these spoken words from the diary using speech verbs between the two statements.

E.g. *'They've got the crowd behind them now,'* <u>*Dad muttered.*</u> *'I think we're in trouble.'*

Manager's Message
Use the example to notice the punctuation you need to change.

a) 'Dive! _____ It was a dive!'
b) 'Never mind. _____ They played their best, didn't they?'

Skills Practice 2

Rewrite these sentences using alternative verbs for *said*.

a) 'I think we're in trouble,' _____ Dad.
b) 'He dived!' _____ Joe.
c) 'I can't look,' _____ Fran.
d) 'I think you're right,' _____ Jim.
e) 'On no!' he _____.
f) 'We're going to Wembley!' we all _____.

Manager's Message
Always using *said* as a speech verb can lead to dull writing.

Game On

Answer these questions with full sentences.

1. Where was the semi-final being played?
2. Who went with Fran to watch the match?
3. What did Dad think in extra time and why?
4. Why did Jim say, 'Never mind' before the game was over?
5. Fran said, 'It was the best night ever.' Write three other sentences to describe her thoughts and feelings.

http://www.shelby.premiumtv.co.uk/

Logon   Contact A Creative   BBC NEWS | ... Front Page   Demon Inter...Mail: Login   eBay UK – T...Marketplace

F⚽TIE TALK

Home

News

Message board

Contact us

TODAY'S THREAD:

__If you had to choose between the two, would you want Premier League survival or Carling Cup glory for Shelby Town this season?__

Comment by ST*TILL*I*DIE
Posted 42 minutes ago

Wembley will be beautiful but I want to be in the Premier League next year. All that matters is the TV money and Town moving forward. I'll be grateful if we finish 4th from bottom!

Comment by northstandgus
Posted 37 minutes ago

Has anybody realised that we will be in Europe next season? As long as Arsenal finish top four, we will be in the UEFA Cup even if they beat us! So, let's stay up!!!

Comment by ShelbyNYNY
Posted 34 minutes ago

Just wanted you guys to know there will be five of us flying from the US to be at Wembley on Sunday. We're thankful! Now when we tell people here that we support Shelby Town, they don't just say, 'WHO?' Now you're gonna believe us. WE'RE GOING TO WIN THE CUP!

Comment by ST*TILL*I*DIE
Posted 25 minutes ago

All the way from New York? Shelby's everywhere these days. Enjoy the trip, boys. But we're here every week and we want to be watching Town in the Premier League! Anyway, why can't we win the Cup and stay up???!

Comment by GeordieST
Posted 23 minutes ago

Why not, eh? Arsenal will be playing their youth team again. Northstandgus is wrong about the UEFA Cup, though. We've got to win to be in. So: COME ON TOWN!!

ST*TILL*I*DIE   SHELBY NY   Geordie ST

Team Talk:
🛡 Read the names of the people who posted messages.
Work out what they are in full.
🛡 What would you call yourself as a Shelby Town supporter?

Skills Practice 1

Find 'beautiful' in the message board comments. *Beautiful* is an adjective.

a) Find and copy another adjective in the text that ends with the suffix *-ful*.

b) Write five more adjectives ending *-ful*.

Skills Practice 2

List six adjectives ending *-ful*. Write a sentence for each.

E.g. *Football is sometimes called 'The beautiful game'.*

Write three different adjectives to replace 'beautiful' in this sentence.

Manager's Message
Adjectives add information to nouns.

Game On

Answer these questions with full sentences.

1. How many people posted messages in the thread? Write their names.
2. Which Cup might Shelby Town play in next season?
3. Where does ShelbyNY live? How do you know?
4. Would ST*TILL*I*DIE prefer Shelby to win the Carling Cup or stay in the Premiership? Why?
5. Make up a name and write a comment of your own that you could add to the thread.

SPORT

February 27th • Daily News

BRAVE SHELBY CRASH TO ARSENAL

Class Tells In Final Minutes At Wembley

New Wembley but a real old-fashioned Cup Final. After 90 minutes of blood and sweat, cheers for Arsenal and tears for Shelby Town. But what a match! 4-1 may sound like it was easy for the Gunners. In fact, Arsenal's talented kids had to fight every step of the way. The Carling Cup wasn't won until Arsene Wenger put on some of his big names late in the game.

For 75 minutes the Premier League new boys matched the odds-on favourites and gave us an afternoon to remember. In fact, for 20 minutes before half-time it looked like a shock was on the cards. Dotun Odegbame has been one of the buys of the season and put Shelby ahead with a great shot from the edge of the box. If Town could have hung on then, who knows? But right on half-time, midfielder Fran Merida volleyed in to equalise for Arsenal.

Fans of both teams probably thought the Gunners would come out firing for the second half. Armand Traore got forward and had Shelby keeper Jim MacDonald scrambling to push away a low cross. But then, at the other end, it took a fabulous fingertip save from Lukasz Fabianski in the Arsenal goal to deny Danny Smith. For twenty-five minutes, it was end to end stuff. Anybody's game.

With extra time looming, though, Arsenal made their changes. They made all the difference. With his first touch after coming on, Theo Walcott slipped between two Shelby defenders and jabbed the ball past MacDonald. Then, Robin Van Persie bent a free kick from 22 yards into the top corner and the Cup was won. Town had fought so hard and the 4-1 scoreline was tough on them when Van Persie poached his second in injury time.

Arsenal grabbed the silverware but the glory belonged to Shelby Town. The Gunners are back in Champions League action next week. For Shelby, it's back to the serious business of staying in the Premier League.

Team Talk:

🛡 In pairs, take turns to summarise each alternate paragraph in three or fewer sentences.

🛡 Remember to look for the main points when you are summarising.

Skills Practice 1

Change these present tense irregular verbs into the past tense. Write them down.
E.g. *is* ⟶ *was*

a) have
b) fight
c) give
d) get
e) take
f) make
g) bend

Manager's Message
Look in the text for help.

Game On

Answer these questions with full sentences.

Skills Practice 2

Rewrite these sentences using more interesting and varied verbs to replace *kicked* each time.

a) He kicked the ball the length of the pitch.
b) He kicked the ball over the keeper's head.
c) He kicked the ball between the defender's legs.
d) He kicked the ball to the man next to him.
e) He went down as the ball was kicked straight into his face.
f) He kicked the ball in with the lightest of touches.

Change this sentence into the past tense.

Walcott doubles Arsenal's lead when he runs onto a ball from Eduardo and places it into the back of the net.

1. What was the final score of the match?
2. Who scored the third goal for Arsenal?
3. Write a definition of the phrase 'Anybody's game'.
4. Why does the reporter describe the result as 'tough' on Shelby Town?
5. Is this a balanced account of the match or a biased one? Give three examples to support your opinion.

Match-day programme Shelby Town v Portsmouth, March 21, Kick-off 7.45

March 21

The Diamond vision

Good evening. Welcome to Manor Park and welcome to our friends from Portsmouth Football Club.

I've been in football for thirty-five years now: as a player, a coach and a manager. If I've learnt one thing, it's this: just when you think you've got it all worked out, just when you think everything's going smoothly, that's when the game comes along and gives you a kick up the backside.

The Carling Cup Final was a great day out: for the players, the club and the supporters. At the time it seemed like we'd cracked it, didn't it? In our first Cup Final and sitting comfortably mid-table in the Premier League. What could possibly go wrong?

I had no complaints about the Final. We gave Arsenal a proper game, never mind the final score. The players were a credit to Shelby Town and so were the fans. Since Wembley, though, four straight defeats have got us into real trouble. Look closely at the Premier League table. See what I mean about a kick up the backside?

What the players have to remember is what we all knew back in August. We had a battle on our hands to stay up. Right now, the table tells us we're still in a battle. We have to get back to doing what we did early in the season. Not giving the ball away. Working hard to get it back. Concentrating hard from first minute to last. We may not be the best team in the Premier League, but we can be the bravest.

Portsmouth have had a difficult season, too. But they know all about getting out of relegation trouble. They've done it successfully in the past. We've got to learn as we go along. Starting tonight. Get behind the boys. You can really make a difference!

Up the Town!

Mick Diamond

Team Talk:
- What do you think the manager's purpose is in writing this message in a match programme?
- What does your own team do to welcome other teams and their supporters?

Skills Practice 1

Copy out these phrases and sentences. Draw a line to link the adverb to the verb it affects.

E.g. *Everything is going smoothly.*

a) They are sitting comfortably mid-table in the League.
b) What could possibly go wrong?
c) Look closely at the League table.
d) Working hard to get it back.
e) You can really make a difference.

Game On

Skills Practice 2

Choose an adverb of your own to describe each of the verbs in these sentences. Copy out the completed sentences.

a) He ran _____ up the wing.
b) The crowd cheered _____.
c) He blew the whistle _____.
d) The captain glared _____ at him.
e) He strode _____ over to the linesman.
f) He _____ held up the cup.

Add an adverb for each verb in this sentence.

He placed the ball on the spot, walked back, then scored the first penalty of the shoot-out.

Answer these questions with full sentences.

1. What two other roles has Mick Diamond had in football?
2. What position in the League were Shelby Town when they were in the Cup Final?
3. Look at paragraph three. Choose the best word to describe how they were feeling: a) cautious b) confident c) critical.
4. What does Mick mean by 'a kick up the backside'?
5. What have Shelby got to learn in this game?

Joe Watson
Year 8

Homework topic, April 14
A difficult situation

Shelby Town were playing Chelsea at Manor Park last Saturday. Chelsea are going for the title and we are in a battle against relegation. It was a difficult situation.

Me, Fran, Mum and Uncle Jim have season tickets, so we could go. I was so nervous that Jim took me to the stadium early and we were almost the first ones there. Before kick-off the atmosphere was electric. Mum and Fran nearly missed the start because the queues outside were so long.

I always think Shelby will win, but on Saturday I was worried. Chelsea looked so sure of themselves. Their players even looked bigger than ours! Our new goalkeeper Jim MacDonald made two saves. Then John Terry scored with a header from the corner and we were a goal down. A difficult situation had got even worse! The Chelsea fans were singing 'Going down, going down!'

The manager, Mick Diamond, must have said something at half-time. Shelby came out and attacked Chelsea non-stop. We hit the bar and Ashley Cole cleared off the line. Then, just as we were thinking it was going to finish 1-0, we scored. The ball came over and Dotun Odegbame flicked it past Peter Cech. We were all going mad but then Mum saw that Dotun was still down.

Heading the ball in, Dotun had crashed into the post and was hurt. He had to go off on a stretcher. Who will score the goals to keep us in the Premier League? We drew with Chelsea. It was a fantastic result, but what will we do without our star striker?

Team Talk:
- With a partner, identify any words in the text that you might find difficult to spell.
- Has your team been in a difficult situation this season? Describe what happened.

Skills Practice 1

Look through the text opposite and find these words:

a) situation
b) could
c) queues
d) Diamond
e) stretcher
f) league

Write them out and circle the tricky bits.

Find a way to remember how to spell each one.

Skills Practice 2

Practise spelling these words using Look Say Cover Write Check.

a) Manor
b) Saturday
c) nervous
d) first
e) atmosphere
f) relegation

Manager's Message
A mnemonic is a way that helps us remember how to spell tricky words, e.g. *'When too means more it has more 'o's.'*

Game On

Answer these questions with full sentences.

1. Why did Joe go to the match early?
2. Why did Mum and Fran nearly miss the start?
3. Why wasn't Joe sure Shelby Town would win?
4. What did the Chelsea fans mean when they sang 'Going down!'?
5. What do you think Mick Diamond said at half-time?

NOW SPORTS

BREAKING NEWS: ODEGBAME OUT

April 14

Presenter: So, after the international break, it's back to Premier League action tomorrow. Let's catch up on some team news now. We'll start at Shelby Town where manager Mick Diamond has a problem upfront. Nick Collins is at Manor Park.

Nick Collins: Yes, thanks Rob. The Shelby manager is with me. Some bad news for you today, Mick?

Mick Diamond: That's right, Nick. It looks like Dotun Odegbame is going to be out for a month. Maybe more. We hoped he would be OK if he had a couple of weeks' rest. He wasn't able to go off to play for Nigeria. But his shoulder was still painful so we got him in for a scan. There is a tear in the muscle between his shoulder and his collar bone. There is nothing they can do so he'll just have to wait for it to heal.

Nick: He left the ground with his arm in a sling.

Mick: That's to take the weight off it. He could do more damage if his arm moves around too much.

Nick: So what will you do at the Madejski on Sunday?

Mick: Well, as you know, Tom Allenby is just back from injury himself. But we'll need some experience against Reading so I'm going to throw him straight back in. We know Tom will give it everything. I'm going to put a youngster on the bench. I'd say Stuart Dolan is a season or two away from the first team but he'll be there if we need him. He's only 17 but he's a level-headed lad. It'll be good experience for him if nothing else.

Nick: How worried are you, Mick? In a relegation battle you need your best players, don't you?

Mick: I'll tell you after Sunday!

Presenter: Thanks Mick. Thanks Nick. Remember: Reading versus Shelby is live this Sunday from 1.30pm, followed by Liverpool versus Arsenal at 4.00pm.

Team Talk:
- In groups of three, read the TV Sports News, each taking one of the roles.
- Who is your favourite TV football presenter? Why?

Skills Practice 1

Rewrite these simple sentences using *if* or *so* to link them.

a) We hoped he would be OK. He had a couple of weeks' rest.

b) His shoulder was still painful. We got him in for a scan.

c) There is nothing they can do. He'll just have to wait for it to heal.

d) We'll need some experience against Reading. I'm going to throw him straight back in.

e) He'll be there. We need him.

f) It'll be good experience for him. Nothing else.

Now find the sentences in the text to check your answers.

Skills Practice 2

Rewrite these sentences using a different past tense verb for the verbs and verb-phrases that are in bold print.

E.g. *He **wasn't able to** go off to play for Nigeria.*
*He **couldn't** go off to play for Nigeria.*

a) We **got him in** for a scan.

b) How **worried** are you, Mick?

c) He **had** a couple of weeks' rest.

d) His shoulder **was still** painful.

Game On

Answer these questions with full sentences.

1. For how long will Dotun be out of the game?

2. What is Dotun's injury?

3. Has Tom Allenby played for Shelby before? Give a reason for your answer.

4. Explain the phrase 'It'll be good experience for him *if nothing else*.'

5. Why do you think Mick tells the interviewer that he'll 'tell him after Sunday'?

April 18

Dear Mum and Dad,

Hi. How are you? I'm sorry if you got a bit of a shock when you heard I wouldn't be coming to Lagos for the Nigeria game. For a couple of days after the Chelsea match I didn't know what was happening. My shoulder hurt but I thought it would go away. When it didn't, the physio was very strict with me: 'Unless you take it easy, you will do more damage, Dotun.' He sounded like you when I was a little boy, Mum!

Anyway, now we know what is wrong. I just have to wait and hope I can play again this season. You know that I am very happy at the club and I wanted to score goals to make sure Shelby stay in the Premier League. People have been saying: 'Oh, they will go down unless Odegbame is fit.' It's good that they think I am an important player in England but it is more important that Shelby do well.

I had to watch the game against Reading on TV on Sunday. The guy who played instead of me, Tom Allenby, did well. He works very hard for the team even though he is not 100% fit. It was a great game to win, even if the goal was a bit lucky. We have had enough bad luck, haven't we?

We have two home games now. I know I will not play but I will go along to cheer the boys. If we could win them both I think we will be safe. I don't know what the manager will do. Perhaps he will play the young striker who came on at the end on Sunday. I have talked to him and he is a very confident young player. Maybe he will get his chance tomorrow night against Spurs.

When my arm is not so sore the manager has said I can come home to visit for a few days. I will tell you when..

Your son,

Dotun

Team Talk:
- What news does Dotun tell his parents?
- In pairs, use the cartoon strip as a prompt to retell the news in Dotun's letter. Try to use as much detail as you can.

Skills Practice 1

Rewrite these sentences using *unless* to begin them.

E.g. *Unless you do your homework first, you can't go out.*

a) I'll be late home unless the practice is cancelled.
b) We will go down unless we win this game.
c) You can borrow my boots unless they're too small.
d) You'll do more harm unless you rest your knee.
e) We'll struggle to win unless our captain can play.

Skills Practice 2

Choose the best connective for the sentences below using: *although*, *if*, *unless*. Write out the complete sentences.

a) We won the game, _____ the team struggled.
b) We will lose _____ we score in extra time.
c) They will win _____ we don't get this penalty.
d) I'll be a sub _____ I might not get on the pitch.
e) Check with the coach _____ you aren't sure.
f) We are bound to lose _____ Dotun plays.

Game On

Answer these questions with full sentences.

1. Why does Dotun want to score goals?
2. Who sounded like Dotun's mum?
3. Why might Dotun's parents have been shocked when he didn't go to Lagos?
4. Explain what the sentence 'People think they will go down' means.
5. Think of two reasons why Dotun might want to go home.

April 19

Shelby Town's hero?

Stuart Dolan bent down to tie up the laces on his boots. He was very nervous. Looking down, he didn't have to look around the dressing room at his team-mates. He had never felt excitement to match this. Here he was, thirty minutes away from making his full debut for Shelby Town. At 7.45pm the whistle would blow and he'd be starting a first team game for the first time. The ground was already full for Spurs at home. Ledley King, the Spurs captain and one of the best defenders in the world, was going to be waiting for him!

Stuart had come on for ten minutes at the end of Sunday's game at Reading. He'd run around like crazy, trying to make an impression. Shelby had spent most of that time in their own half, desperately trying to hang onto their one-goal lead. He'd joined in the celebrations at the end, but somehow the whole thing had passed him by. It had all been a bit like a dream.

Nothing had been said since, except for Tom Appleby nudging him at training and saying: 'You did all right there, son.' Today after training, though, the gaffer had pulled him to one side:

'I've got some news for you, Stuart,' Mick Diamond had told him. 'You're starting against Tottenham tonight.'

Stuart had felt dizzy for a moment, almost as if he was going to be sick. But he'd gulped hard and just mumbled,

'Thanks, boss. I won't let you down.'

'I know you won't, son.'

Stuart pulled his second lace tight, took a deep breath and sat up straight. Outside, he could hear them announcing the Shelby Town team.

'Up front with Tom Appleby tonight will be number 22, Stuart Dolan.'

He could hear the fans cheer. Then, suddenly, the bell rang. Dave Morgan stood up and clapped his hands. He looked over at Stuart.

'Come on, son. This is it. You're going to be Shelby Town's hero tonight!'

Team Talk:
- Read paragraph three from 'Nothing had been said...' up to 'I know you won't, son.'
- Talk with a partner about how Stuart must have felt, what he thought and what he might have done.

Skills Practice 1

Use Look Say Cover Write Check to practise spelling these one-syllable words.

a) team
b) goal
c) half
d) dream
e) since
f) breath

Manager's Message
Breaking longer words into syllables can help you remember their spellings.

Game On

Skills Practice 2

Use Look Say Cover Write Check to practise these multi-syllabic words.

a) excitement
b) minutes
c) already
d) impression
e) desperately
f) celebrations

Practise spelling the names of these football grounds. Which team plays at each one?

a) Emirates Stadium
b) Craven Cottage
c) Villa Park
d) Ewood Park
e) White Hart Lane

Answer these questions with full sentences.

1. How long does Stuart have to wait before making his first team debut?
2. When did Stuart learn he was going to play from the beginning of the Spurs match?
3. Why do you think Stuart was looking down in the changing room?
4. Why did Stuart feel dizzy?
5. What effect do you think the word 'hero' had on Stuart?

Welcome back to Ford Wednesday Night Football on TalkSport. Don't forget you'll be able to have your say on the phone-in that starts at 10pm. And there'll be plenty to talk about, won't there? Arsenal and Manchester United march on in the Champions League and Chelsea take another big step towards winning the title. They're three points clear with a game in hand after that win against Liverpool at Stamford Bridge. But maybe the best story of the night was at Manor Park. Let's cross there now and talk to Shelby manager Mick Diamond.

The best story of the night

talkSP[OR]

A new Manor Park hero

Stuart gave Ledley a really hard game

MANSION

Thanks for joining us, Mick.

Good evening, Ian.

A very good evening for you, Mick. 2-1 winners over Spurs. Are you safe?

Oh, I don't know about that. There's still a long way to go this season. But it was an important win, that's for sure.

And a new hero for the Manor Park faithful?

Oh, never mind the fans, Ian. Stuart Dolan's a new hero for his team-mates! He's getting mobbed in the dressing room!

Do you get the credit for giving him a game?

No, all the credit goes to the boy himself. He knows that if it wasn't for the injury to Dotun, he wouldn't have got a chance. But now he has and he's grabbed it, hasn't he?

Am I right in thinking that Dolan is Shelby's youngest ever league scorer?

I don't know, Ian. I'll leave the stats to you media boys. All I'd say is that Stuart was up against a great player tonight in Ledley King and he's given him a really hard game.

So will he play against Bolton at the weekend?

Well, after tonight, I can't really leave the boy out, can I?

Thanks for talking to us, Mick. The Shelby Town manager, talking about the scorer of the opening goal at Manor Park tonight. Stuart Dolan, I can confirm, is the youngest player to score a league goal in the club's history. Congratulations to him. We're off to Old Trafford next with Ford on TalkSport.

Team Talk:
- Use the text as a model to role-play an interview with Stuart Dolan instead of the manager.
- Which Premier League manager would you most like to interview and why?

Skills Practice 1

Replace the underlined nouns with pronouns: *they/them/their*; *he/him/his*; *it/its*. Write out the new sentences.

a) Stuart scored <u>Stuart's</u> first goal tonight.

b) The players played <u>the players'</u> best game.

c) Tell Mick I will meet <u>Mick</u> later.

d) The keeper watched the ball as <u>the ball</u> slammed into the net.

e) The team gasped at the ref as <u>the ref</u> held up a red card.

f) The fans cheered at the top of <u>the fans'</u> voices.

Game On

Skills Practice 2

List the pronouns in each of these phrases. Find them in the text opposite and identify the nouns they refer to.

E.g. *for his team mates.*
     his. Stuart Dolan.

a) He's getting mobbed ...

b) ... Dotun, he wouldn't have ...

c) ... he's given him a really ...

d) So will he play ...

e) Congratulations to him.

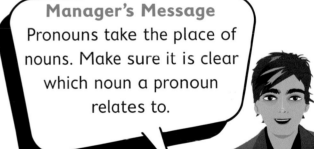

Manager's Message
Pronouns take the place of nouns. Make sure it is clear which noun a pronoun relates to.

Answer these questions with full sentences.

1. Who is the presenter on TalkSport talking to in the first paragraph of the text?
2. What does Mick Diamond call the presenter?
3. Why does Mick say 'There's a long way to go this season'?
4. Who does the interviewer mean by 'the Manor Park faithful'?
5. Will Stuart be playing in the next match? Give a reason for your answer.

Match-day programme

April 23

According to the skipper

Sammy's a great coach

Stuart's a sensible lad

LOCAL HERO
Shelby Town's Stuart Dolan

Your support's been great this season!

Well, I hope you've got your breath back after Wednesday night. I can tell you there's one boy around Shelby whose feet haven't touched the floor yet!

First of all, I should say welcome to Manor Park to the players, staff and supporters of Bolton Wanderers. Especially their manager, who I worked with on Under-21 duty many years ago. He's a great coach and a great bloke. I think he was the first person on the phone to me to say 'Well done' after we won promotion last season. I hope he'll have to say the same thing to me after the game tonight!

I've got to say a word about young Stuart Dolan. Stuart's already in the history books thanks to his goal against Spurs. There's been a lot of fuss made of him the last couple of days. He won't let that go to his head, though. He's a sensible lad and I hope his goal the other night will be the first of many in a Shelby Town shirt. Stuart is still learning the game but Wednesday wasn't a bad start!

I know people have been saying that a win today will secure our place in the Premier League for another season. The manager just keeps telling us to try to get what we can from every game. You can't be sure until the points on the board mean you're absolutely safe. On the other hand, we mustn't go into today's game thinking that, if we don't win, we're going to be relegated. We just have to find a couple of victories between now and the end of the season.

Your support has been great all season. I never thought I'd see Manor Park full for every home game. It's another big night for us tonight. Get behind us, whatever happens!

Up the Town!

Dave Morgan

Team Talk:

🛡 In pairs, identify the main point of each paragraph in the text.

🛡 What is the main thing you would say about your team's next match?

Skills Practice 1

Adverbs add detail and interest to action verbs. Most adverbs end in *-ly*, but watch out for exceptions. Identify which of the following sentences use an adverb and which use an adjective. Write the adverbs and adjectives in two lists.

a) He ran rapidly after the ball.
b) He scored a magnificent goal.
c) Despite trying hard, he couldn't keep up.
d) The manager gave a spirited half-time talk.
e) He gently gave the ball a tap out of play.
f) Study the game-plan carefully.

Skills Practice 2

Rewrite these sentences adding an adverb.

a) He ran onto the pitch.
b) The crowd cheered.
c) The manager frowned when it happened.
d) He fell to the ground.
e) They were panting by the end of the first half.

Identify the adverbs in this paragraph.

United, at home, were repeatedly outplayed by the Birmingham side until the second half. Then they attacked ferociously and showed the visitors how they could really play.

Game On

Answer these questions with full sentences.

1. Who are Shelby Town about to play against?
2. Why does the captain especially welcome Bolton's manager?
3. 'There's one boy ... whose feet haven't touched the floor.' Who is the captain referring to and what does he mean?
4. Why has Stuart made the history books?
5. What is the purpose of this programme page?

April 2008

28 Friday

Two games to go. Where will Shelby be in two weeks' time? Still in the Premier League or back in the Championship? I really do think we're going to stay up. It would all have been easier if we had beaten Bolton last weekend. It looked like we were on our way: 2-0 up and 20 minutes to go. But football's never that simple. It's why we all love it so much. You never know what's round the corner. Anyway, 2-2 got us one point closer to where we want to be. And none of the clubs below us won, either. I hate maths at school but I've been sitting at home, working out all the points and games and goals for and against every night this week!

Jim's taking us to Newcastle tomorrow for the game. Just me and Joe because Dad's got to work. We're going on the supporters' club coach because Jim said he didn't want to be doing with directions and parking. After Wembley, St James' Park will be the biggest ground I've been to. They get crowds of about 55,000, which is nearly twice what we can fit inside Manor Park. No wonder they can afford to buy big star players every summer. I'm so proud we can go and give them a game. I bet they'll want revenge now for us beating them at home.

Joe always says he's not bothered about who we're playing. He just wants us to win. But I think one of the best things this season has been seeing the other teams' players. I've been watching football on TV for years and now, every week, I see those players in the flesh. Tomorrow Mark Viduka, Michael Owen and Joey Barton will all be playing for Newcastle. Can Danny Smith and Pierre Vert and Stuart Dolan win us the game? It's great to see us playing against the big stars. Newcastle United versus Shelby Town. I hope we'll be playing them again next season!

Team Talk:
- Talk about what you would put in your diary the night before going to see Newcastle United play your team.
- Which Premier League team would you most like your team to play, and why?

Skills Practice 1

Say these words aloud quickly, as if in a conversation. Find which letters (vowels) are not stressed. Say them again and stress all the letters.

Practise spelling them by using SpeakSpell (e.g. ev-er-ee) and using Look Say Cover Write Check.

a) really
b) every
c) supporters
d) directions
e) bothered

Find a way to remember them.

Skills Practice 2

Look at the letters in these words. What do they have in common?

a) football
b) sitting
c) supporters
d) tomorrow
e) afford
f) summer

Practise spelling these Premier League nicknames.

a) The Gunners   **d)** The Toffees
b) The Trotters   **e)** The Latics
c) The Royals   **f)** Pompey

Write down the correct team name for each of the team nicknames.

Game On

Answer these questions with full sentences.

1. Where could Shelby Town be in two weeks?
2. Why isn't Dad going to Newcastle?
3. Why can Newcastle afford to buy star players and Shelby cannot?
4. What is now different for Fran when she watches football?
5. Fran hopes Shelby Town will be playing against Newcastle next season. How could this happen?

Notes for my report on NEWCASTLE U V SHELBY T (800-1000 words needed)

Sat, 3PM kick off. St James' Park. Att. 53,497

Windy afternoon. Weather fair. Ground almost full. Noisy Away crowd (5000) up in top tier of corner stand. ST need win to guarantee survival. Maybe a point will do, depending on other results. Home crowd flat because NU have missed out on European place. Big cheers for Mark Viduka when he warms up. 20 goals for season. A man to replace Shearer at last!

Morgan wins toss. NU kick off. ST attack Gallowgate End. Take NU by surprise first few minutes. Attacking down wings with Smith and Dunne. Crunch! Vert versus Barton. First tackle. Both need treatment after. FK ST. Allenby heads wide. Dolan takes on Taylor by corner flag. Nutmeg. Cheers from ST fans!

NU take charge after 20 mins. Owen tripped by Morgan. Viduka FK just wide. Lots of possession but few chances. NU fans gets restless. To half-time: lots of mistakes both sides. Scrappy. ST nervous, need result. NU nervous. Why? Crowd? Manager down from Directors' Box, shouting orders.

HT 0-0

ST start again like first half. 55 mins **GOAL 0-1**. Dunne low cross from left. Half-cleared to edge of box. Dolan to Allenby on edge of D. Low shot past Given. Away support goes mental. Home fans roar at last! NU react. 10 mins heavy pressure on ST goal. 67 mins **GOAL 1-1**. Viduka picks up ball 35 yards out, back to goal. Spins marker. Lays pass into box. Owen pounces, 10 yards out. Pokes past MacDonald.

NU press for winner. ST well-organised. Last ten mins, fear takes over. Stalemate. One scare for ST: Morgan back pass caught by wind. MacDonald has to scramble behind for corner.

FT 1-1

NU players take lap of honour, last home game. Good reaction from crowd. But biggest cheer is other results. **Draw means ST are safe!** Away fans celebrate. ST Players come out. Clapped by NU players and by NU fans. Good sports. Great season for ST.

Team Talk:
- With a partner, work out what all the abbreviations mean.
- When do you need to write brief notes?

Skills Practice 1

Rewrite the first paragraph of the report notes using complete sentences and punctuation.

Manager's Message
Change the order and add any extra nouns or verbs you think necessary to make the information clear.

Skills Practice 2

Look at each paragraph of the report notes and identify the main point or points.

Write a summary of the match report notes in one paragraph. E.g. *Paragraph 1: weather, atmosphere*

Write the following match report as brief notes.

Reading won the toss but by half time were one-nil down. The second half saw Reading score twice, but a last-second header from Wigan led to the disappointing full-time result as a draw.

Game On

Answer these questions with full sentences.

1. Describe what the weather was like in one sentence.
2. What was the result of Morgan tripping up Owen?
3. Explain what 'Home crowd flat' means.
4. How did both sets of fans react to the first goal?
5. Explain why the author has written in note form.

May 7

Let's get out there and get stuck in!

With twenty minutes to go before kick-off, there was a hum of excitement in the Shelby Town dressing room. The players could hear the crowd outside, singing,

'Premier League? You're having a laugh!'

Tom Allenby and Dotun Odegbame came over to Stuart Dolan. Dotun shook Stuart's hand.

'Well done, Stuart. I'm fit again but maybe you should have been playing today.'

Dave gave Stuart a nudge.

'Yeah. Look, if the boss doesn't bring you on, I'll pretend to get injured ten minutes before the end!'

Stuart laughed and then looked across the room. The door had opened and the Shelby chairman, Mr Carstairs, stood in front of them. He was smiling and holding a glass of champagne.

'Well done, lads,' he said. 'Great season. Let's celebrate in style this afternoon, eh?'

As soon as he'd left, Danny Smith giggled,

'I think he's already started, hasn't he?'

Everybody laughed. The manager stood up and reminded them there was still a football match to be played.

'Don't let our fans down, eh? Let's finish with three points today. Send everybody off on holiday in the right mood. The chairman's right. It has been a great season. I'm proud of you all. Right attitude this afternoon, though. Next season starts now!'

Finally, Dave Morgan stood up to have his say, too.

'Gaffer's spot on, boys. We've worked really hard this year. Let's make sure we do it again today. Paul Ince will make sure the Blackburn players aren't already thinking about the beach. And if we are, they'll hammer us. Let's get out there and get stuck in!'

Team Talk:

🛡 Think of two adjectives to describe the tone and atmosphere of the text.

🛡 How do you feel as the football season draws to a close?

Skills Practice 1

Rewrite the following as dialogue, using the correct punctuation.

a) Well done Stuart I'm fit again but maybe you should have been playing today said Dotun

b) Yeah Look if the boss doesn't bring you on I'll pretend to get injured ten minutes before the end said Dave

c) I think he's already started hasn't he giggled Danny Smith

Skills Practice 2

Choose your favourite team and write a short speech that its manager might give at the end of the season.

Manager's Message
Check the punctuation of your speech.

Game On

Answer these questions with full sentences.

1. What could the players hear from outside the dressing room?
2. Who came in to say 'Well done'?
3. What had Mr Carstairs already started to do?
4. What mood did the manager want everybody to be in after the match?
5. What do you think the manager would say to the team after the match if they lost or drew?

http://www.shelby.premiumtv.co.uk/ Google

Logon Contact A Creative BBC NEWS | ... Front Page Demon Inter...Mail: Login eBay UK – T...Marketplace

Shelby Town FC

Home

News

Manager's page

Fixtures

Match reports

Online shop

Contact us

VOTE IN OUR END OF SEASON WEBSITE POLL

May 10

WHAT A SEASON!!!

What a party that was on Sunday afternoon! The win, the lap of honour and the fireworks to celebrate a fantastic achievement for the club. Staying up and going to Wembley for the Carling Cup Final. And now the smoke's cleared? We can look forward to another season where Shelby Town belong. Still in the Premier League!

Congratulations to Mick, the players and all the staff. Some of us here haven't got any fingernails left. But we knew you could do it. And you did! Thanks as well to all the supporters who followed Town, home and away, in the club's historic first season in the Premier League. Now's your chance to have your say on the season, with our exclusive website poll.

Just email your votes via the link. We'll bring you the results at the end of May!

SHELBY TOWN WEBSITE POLL

1. *Shelby Town player of the season*
2. *Shelby Town young player of the season*
3. *Best team performance of the season (Home)*
4. *Best team performance of the season (Away)*
5. *Best atmosphere (Home)*
6. *Best atmosphere (Away)*
7. *Goal of the season*
8. *Save of the season*

Just one vote per category, please. And just one vote per supporter! And while you're voting, why not use the **Memories Link** to our great website competition? Be in with a chance of winning lunch at the Far Post Restaurant at Manor Park for you and your mates before a home game next season. We'll even throw in four match tickets! In less than 100 words, describe your best Shelby Town moment of last season. On or off the pitch, funny, dramatic or disappointing, it's up to you. Get thinking now and you could be a winner and start next season in style! The best entry received wins that slap-up meal and tickets for a game next season. We'll feature all our favourite entries on the Shelby Town website over the summer.

Get writing! And 'Come On Town'!

Team Talk: ● Talk about how you would vote on the Shelby Town website poll.
● Does your team have a website? What is it like?